Congressional
Research
Service

Carbon Capture and Sequestration: Research, Development, and Demonstration at the U.S. Department of Energy

Peter Folger

Specialist in Energy and Natural Resources Policy

April 23, 2012

Congressional Research Service

7-5700

www.crs.gov

R42496

CRS Report for Congress
Prepared for Members and Committees of Congress

Summary

On March 27, 2012, the U.S. Environmental Protection Agency (EPA) proposed a new rule that would limit emissions to no more than 1,000 pounds of carbon dioxide (CO_2) per megawatt-hour of production from new fossil-fuel power plants with a capacity of 25 megawatts or larger. EPA proposed the rule under Section 111 of the Clean Air Act. According to EPA, new natural gas-fired combined-cycle power plants should be able to meet the proposed standards without additional cost. However, new coal-fired plants would only be able to meet the standards by installing carbon capture and sequestration (CCS) technology.

The proposed rule has sparked increased scrutiny of the future of CCS as a viable technology for reducing CO_2 emissions from coal-fired power plants. The proposed rule also places a new focus on whether the U.S. Department of Energy's (DOE's) CCS research, development, and demonstration (RD&D) program will achieve its vision of developing an advanced CCS technology portfolio ready by 2020 for large-scale CCS deployment.

Congress has appropriated nearly $6 billion since FY2008 for CCS RD&D at DOE's Office of Fossil Energy: approximately $2.3 billion from annual appropriations and $3.4 billion from the American Recovery and Reinvestment Act (or Recovery Act). The large and rapid influx of funding for industrial-scale CCS projects from the Recovery Act may accelerate development and deployment of CCS in the United States. However, the future deployment of CCS may take a different course if the major components of the DOE program follow a path similar to DOE's flagship CCS demonstration project, FutureGen, which has experienced delays and multiple changes of scope and design since its inception in 2003. A question for Congress is whether FutureGen represents a unique case of a first mover in a complex, expensive, and technically challenging endeavor, or whether it indicates the likely path for all large CCS demonstration projects once they move past the planning stage.

Since enactment of the Recovery Act, DOE has shifted its RD&D emphasis to the demonstration phase of carbon capture technology. The shift appears to heed recommendations from many experts who called for large, industrial-scale carbon capture demonstration projects (e.g., 1 million tons of CO_2 captured per year). Funding from the Recovery Act for large-scale demonstration projects was 40% of the total amount of DOE funding for all CCS RD&D from FY2008 through FY2012.

To date, there are no commercial ventures in the United States that capture, transport, and inject industrial-scale quantities of CO_2 solely for the purposes of carbon sequestration. However, CCS RD&D in 2012 is just now embarking on commercial-scale demonstration projects for CO_2 capture, injection, and storage. The success of these projects will likely bear heavily on the future outlook for widespread deployment of CCS technologies as a strategy for preventing large quantities of CO_2 from reaching the atmosphere while U.S. power plants continue to burn fossil fuels, mainly coal.

Given the pending EPA rule, congressional interest in the future of coal as a domestic energy source appears directly linked to the future of CCS. In the short term, congressional support for building new coal-fired power plants could be expressed through legislative action to modify or block the proposed EPA rule. Alternatively, congressional oversight of the CCS RD&D program could help inform decisions about the level of support for the program and help Congress gauge whether it is on track to meet its goals.

Contents

Figures

Tables

Contacts

Introduction

Carbon capture and sequestration (or storage)—known as CCS—is a physical process that involves capturing manmade carbon dioxide (CO_2) at its source and storing it before its release to the atmosphere. CCS could reduce the amount of CO_2 emitted to the atmosphere while allowing the continued use of fossil fuels at power plants and other large, industrial facilities. An integrated CCS system would include three main steps: (1) capturing CO_2 at its source and separating it from other gases; (2) purifying, compressing, and transporting the captured CO_2 to the sequestration site; and (3) injecting the CO_2 into subsurface geological reservoirs. Following its injection into a subsurface reservoir, the CO_2 would need to be monitored for leakage and to verify that it remains in the target geological reservoir. Once injection operations cease, a responsible party would need to take title to the injected CO_2 and ensure that it stays underground in perpetuity.

The U.S. Department of Energy (DOE) has pursued research and development of aspects of the three main steps leading to an integrated CCS system since 1997.[1] Congress has appropriated nearly $6 billion since FY2008 for CCS research, development, and demonstration (RD&D) at DOE's Office of Fossil Energy: approximately $2.3 billion in total annual appropriations, and $3.4 billion from the American Recovery and Reinvestment Act (P.L. 111-5, enacted February 17, 2009, hereinafter referred to as the Recovery Act).

The large and rapid influx of funding for industrial-scale CCS projects from the Recovery Act may accelerate development and demonstration of CCS in the United States, particularly if the RD&D pursued by DOE's CCS program achieves its goals as outlined in the department's 2010 RD&D *CCS Roadmap*.[2] However, the future deployment of CCS may take a different course if the major components of the DOE program follow a path similar to DOE's FutureGen project, which has experienced delays and multiple changes of scope and design since its inception in 2003.

This report aims to provide a snapshot of the DOE CCS program, including its current funding levels and the budget request for FY2013, together with some discussion of the program's achievements and prospects for success in meeting its stated goals. Other CRS reports provide substantial detail on the technological aspects of CCS (CRS Report R41325, *Carbon Capture: A Technology Assessment*), general information on the different components of CCS and their advantages and disadvantages (CRS Report RL33801, *Carbon Capture and Sequestration (CCS)*), and information on various challenges to CCS deployment (CRS Report RL34621, *Capturing CO2 from Coal-Fired Power Plants: Challenges for a Comprehensive Strategy*, and CRS Report RL34601, *Community Acceptance of Carbon Capture and Sequestration Infrastructure: Siting Challenges*).

---

[1] U.S. Department of Energy, National Energy Technology Laboratory, *Carbon Sequestration Program Technology Program Plan*, Enhancing the Success of Carbon Capture and Storage Technologies, February 2011, p. 10, http://www.netl.doe.gov/technologies/carbon_seq/refshelf/2011_Sequestration_Program_Plan.pdf.

[2] U.S. Department of Energy, National Energy Technology Laboratory, *DOE/NETL Carbon Dioxide Capture and Storage RD&D Roadmap*, December 2010, http://www.netl.doe.gov/technologies/carbon_seq/refshelf/ CCSRoadmap.pdf. Hereinafter referred to as the DOE 2010 *CCS Roadmap*.

Issues for Congress

EPA Proposed Rule Limiting CO₂ Emissions from Power Plants

On March 27, 2012, the U.S. Environmental Protection Agency (EPA) proposed a new rule that would limit emissions from new fossil-fuel power plants to no more than 1,000 pounds of CO_2 per megawatt-hour of energy produced. It would apply to plants with a generating capacity of greater than 25 megawatts.[3] EPA proposed the rule under Section 111 of the Clean Air Act, amending 40 C.F.R. Part 60. According to EPA, new natural gas-fired combined-cycle power plants should be able to meet the proposed standards without additional cost. However, new coal-fired plants would only be able to meet the standards by using CCS.[4]

The proposed rule has sparked increased scrutiny of the future of CCS as a viable technology for reducing CO_2 emissions from coal-fired power plants. The proposed rule also places a new focus on DOE's CCS RD&D program—whether it will achieve its vision of "having an advanced CCS technology portfolio ready by 2020 for large-scale CCS demonstration that provides for the safe, cost-effective carbon management that will meet our Nation's goals for reducing [greenhouse gas] emissions."[5]

On March 27, 2012, EPA Administrator Lisa Jackson reportedly stated that CCS would be commercially available within 10 years.[6] Further, EPA's regulatory impact analysis, which accompanied the proposed rule, stated that "EPA intends this rule to send a clear signal about the future of CCS technology that, in conjunction with other policies such as Department of Energy (DOE) financial assistance, the agency estimates will support development and demonstration of CCS technology from coal-fired plants at commercial scale, if that financial assistance is made available under appropriate market conditions."[7]

The prospects for building new coal-fired electricity generating plants depend on many factors, such as costs of competing fuel sources (e.g., natural gas), electricity demand, regulatory costs, infrastructure (including rail) and electric grid development, and others. However, the EPA proposed rule clearly identifies CCS as the essential technology required if new coal-fired power plants are to be built in the United States.[8]

---

[3] EPA Fact Sheet: *Proposed Carbon Pollution Standard for New Power Plants*, http://epa.gov/carbonpollutionstandard/pdfs/20120327factsheet.pdf.

[4] Ibid. According to EPA, new power plants that use CCS would have the option to use a 30-year average of CO_2 emissions to meet the standard, rather than meeting the annual standard each year. Under this option, new plants would be allowed to emit 1,800 pounds per megawatt-hour for the first 10 years of operation (a standard that should be achievable by an efficient supercritical coal-fired facility or an integrated gasification combined-cycle plant), provided that the facility committed to a 600 pound per megawatt-hour standard for the following 20 years of operation.

[5] DOE 2010 *CCS Roadmap*, p. 3.

[6] Andrew Childers, Bloomberg BNA, "EPA Carbon Rule for Utilities Expected to Continue Trend Toward Natural Gas Plants," March 28, 2012, http://www.bna.com/epa-carbon-rule-n12884908631/.

[7] U.S. Environmental Protection Agency, *Regulatory Impact Analysis for the Proposed Standard of Performance for Greenhouse Gas Emissions for New Stationary Sources*, Electric Utility Generating Units, March 2012, pp. ES3-ES4, http://epa.gov/carbonpollutionstandard/pdfs/20120327proposalRIA.pdf.

[8] The proposed rule is for new power plants, and exempts existing power plants as well as plants that make "modifications" as defined under EPA's New Source Performance Standards. See 40 C.F.R. Part 60.

Congress has appropriated funding for DOE to pursue CCS research and development since 1997 and recently acknowledged the importance of CCS technology by awarding $3.4 billion from the Recovery Act to CCS programs at DOE. Given the pending EPA rule, congressional interest in the future of coal as a domestic energy source appears directly linked to the future of CCS. In the short term, congressional support for building new coal-fired power plants could be expressed through legislative action to modify or block the proposed EPA rule. Alternatively, congressional oversight of the DOE CCS RD&D program could help inform decisions about the level of support for the program and help Congress gauge whether the program is on track to meet its goals. Despite Administrator Jackson's assurances that CCS will be commercially available in 10 years, the history of CCS RD&D at DOE and the pathway of some its signature programs, such as FutureGen, invite questions about whether the RD&D results will enable widespread deployment of CCS in the United States within the next decade.

Legislation

Although DOE has pursued aspects of CCS RD&D since 1997, the Energy Policy Act of 2005 (P.L. 109-58) provided a 10-year authorization for the basic framework of CCS research and development at DOE.[9] The Energy Independence and Security Act of 2007 (EISA, P.L. 110-140) amended the Energy Policy Act of 2005 to include, among other provisions, authorization for seven large-scale CCS demonstration projects (in addition to FutureGen) that would integrate the carbon capture, transportation, and sequestration steps.[10] (Large-scale demonstration programs and their potential significance are discussed below.) It can be argued that, since enactment of EISA, the focus and funding within the CCS RD&D program has shifted towards large-scale capture technology development through these and other demonstration projects.

In addition to the annual appropriations provided for CCS RD&D, the legislation most significant to federal CCS RD&D program activities since passage of EISA has been the Recovery Act (P.L. 111-5). As discussed below, $3.4 billion in funding from the Recovery Act was intended to expand and accelerate the commercial deployment of CCS technologies to allow for commercial-scale demonstration in both new and retrofitted power plants and industrial facilities by 2020.

In the 111th Congress, two bills that would have authorized a national cap-and-trade system for limiting the emission of greenhouse gases (H.R. 2454 and S. 1733) also would have created programs aimed at accelerating the commercial availability of CCS. The programs would have generated funding from a surcharge on electricity delivered from the combustion of fossil fuels— approximately $1 billion per year—and made the funding available for grants, contracts, and financial assistance to eligible entities seeking to develop CCS technology. Another source of funding in the bills was to come from a program that would distribute emission allowances to "early movers," entities that installed CCS technology on up to a total of 20 gigawatts generating capacity. The House of Representatives passed H.R. 2454, but neither bill was enacted.

In the 112th Congress, a few bills have been introduced that would address aspects of CCS RD&D. The Department of Energy Carbon Capture and Sequestration Program Amendments Act

---

[9] P.L. 109-58, Title IX, Subtitle F, §963; 42 U.S.C. 16293.

[10] P.L. 110-140, Title VII, Subtitles A and B.

of 2011 (S. 699) would provide federal indemnification of up to $10 billion per project to early adopters of CCS technology (large CCS demonstration projects).[11]

The New Manhattan Project for Energy Independence (H.R. 301) would create a system of grants and prizes for a variety of technologies, including CCS, that would contribute to reducing U.S. dependence on foreign sources of energy. Other bills introduced would provide tax incentives for the use of CO_2 in enhanced oil recovery (S. 1321), or would eliminate the minimum capture requirement for the CO_2 sequestration tax credit (H.R. 1023). Other bills were also introduced that would affect other aspects of CCS RD&D financing, such as loan guarantees. To date, none of the bills introduced in the 112th Congress affecting federal CCS RD&D, other than annual appropriations, has been enacted.

CCS Research, Development, and Demonstration: Overall Goals

The U.S. Department of Energy states that the mission for the DOE Office of Fossil Energy is "to ensure the availability of ultra-clean (near-zero emissions), abundant, low-cost domestic energy from coal to fuel economic prosperity, strengthen energy security, and enhance environmental quality."[12] Over the past several years, the DOE Fossil Energy Research and Development Program has increasingly shifted activities performed under its Coal Program toward emphasizing CCS as the main focus.[13] The Coal Program itself represented 68% of total Fossil Energy Research and Development appropriations in FY2011 and 75% in FY2012,[14] indicating that CCS has come to dominate coal R&D at DOE. This reflects DOE's view that "there is a growing consensus that steps must be taken to significantly reduce [greenhouse gas] emissions from energy use throughout the world at a pace consistent to stabilize atmospheric concentrations of CO_2, and that CCS is a promising option for addressing this challenge."[15]

DOE also acknowledges that the cost of deploying currently available CCS technologies is very high, and that to be effective as a technology for mitigating greenhouse gas emissions from power plants, the costs for CCS must be reduced.[16] The challenge of reducing the costs of CCS technology is difficult to quantify, in part because there are no examples of currently operating commercial-scale coal-fired power plants equipped with CCS. Nor is it easy to predict when lower-cost CCS technology will be available for widespread deployment in the United States. Nevertheless, DOE observes that "the United States can no longer afford the luxury of

---

[11] Among other provisions, the bill would also amend EISA to expand the number of large CCS demonstration projects from seven to ten.

[12] DOE 2010 *CCS Roadmap*, p. 2.

[13] The Coal Program contains CCS RD&D activities, and is within DOE's Office of Fossil Energy, Fossil Energy Research and Development, as listed in DOE detailed budget justifications for each fiscal year. See, for example, U.S. Department of Energy, FY2013 Congressional Budget Request, volume 3, *Fossil Energy Research and Development*, http://www.cfo.doe.gov/budget/13budget/Content/Volume3.pdf.

[14] U.S. Department of Energy, FY2013 Congressional Budget Request, volume 3, *Fossil Energy Research and Development*, p. 411.

[15] DOE 2010 *CCS Roadmap*, p. 3.

[16] DOE states that the cost of deploying currently available CCS post-combustion technology on a supercritical pulverized coal-fired power plant would increase the cost of electricity by 80%. DOE 2010 *CCS Roadmap*, p. 3.

conventional long-lead times for RD&D to bear results."[17] Thus the coal RD&D program is focused on achieving results that would allow for an advanced CCS technology portfolio to be ready by 2020 for large-scale demonstration.

The following section describes the components of the CCS activities within DOE's coal R&D program and their funding history over the past five fiscal years. This report focuses on this time period because during that time the Recovery Act was enacted and was expected to accelerate the transition of CCS technology to industry for deployment and commercialization.[18]

Program Areas

The 2010 RD&D *CCS Roadmap* described 10 different program areas pursued by DOE's Coal Program within the Office of Fossil Energy: (1) Innovations for Existing Plants (IEP); (2) Advanced Integrated Gasification Combined Cycle (IGCC); (3) Advanced Turbines; (4) Carbon Sequestration; (5) Solid State Energy Conversion Fuel Cells; (6) Fuels; (7) Advanced Research; (8) Clean Coal Power Initiative (CCPI); (9) FutureGen; and (10) Industrial Carbon Capture and Storage Projects (ICCS).[19] **Table 1** shows funding for these program areas through FY2010, including funding provided by the Recovery Act, and for two subprogram areas: (1) Site Characterization, Training, Program Direction; and (2) Carbon Sequestration (Focus Area for CCS Research). DOE changed the program structure after FY2010. **Table 1** reflects those changes and attempts to show how the new program structure matches the old program structure after FY2010.

Some program areas are directly focused on one or more of the three steps of CCS: capture, transportation, and storage. For example, the Carbon Sequestration program area focuses on the third step: evaluating prospective sites for long-term storage of CO_2 underground. In contrast, FutureGen from the outset was envisioned as combining all three steps: a zero-emission fossil fuel plant that would capture its emissions and sequester them in a geologic reservoir.

Other program areas include research that, at first glance, does not seem directly applicable to the three steps of CCS. For example, the CCPI and IEP programs include research aimed at achieving gains in power plant efficiency. These technologies would presumably reduce CO_2 emissions per unit of power generated, even if they were not directly integrated into a carbon capture and sequestration scheme. The DOE *CCS Roadmap* notes that each program area, however, contributes to the overall CCS RD&D effort.

As outlined in the 2010 *CCS Roadmap*, RD&D efforts in several of these program areas overlap. For example, the lead role for pre-combustion carbon capture technology RD&D falls under the Carbon Sequestration program area, but additional pre-combustion technology RD&D also occurs under the IGCC program area and under the Fuels program area.[20] Post-combustion and oxy-combustion carbon capture technology RD&D is conducted in a different program area: IEP, which is focused on technology for new and existing pulverized coal power plants. In addition, the Advanced Research program area conducts research on new breakthrough carbon capture

---

[17] DOE 2010 *CCS Roadmap*, p. 3.

[18] DOE 2010 *CCS Roadmap*, p. 2.

[19] DOE 2010 *CCS Roadmap*, p. 11.

[20] DOE 2010 *CCS Roadmap*, pp. 11-12.

technologies, as does the National Energy Technology Laboratory (NETL) Office of Research and Development (described as external and internal research, respectively, in the 2010 *CCS Roadmap*). Thus, at least six different program areas identified in the 2010 *CCS Roadmap* conduct research on carbon capture technology RD&D.

RD&D is also divided among different industrial sectors in two program areas: the Clean Coal Power Initiative (CCPI) and Industrial Carbon Capture and Storage Projects (ICCS). The CCPI program area focuses on the demonstration phase of carbon capture technology for coal-based power plants. The ICCS area demonstrates carbon capture technology for the non-power plant industrial sector.[21] Both these program areas focus on the *demonstration* component of RD&D, and account for $2.3 billion of the $3.4 billion appropriated for CCS RD&D in the Recovery Act in FY2009. From the budgetary perspective, the Recovery Act funding shifted the emphasis of CCS RD&D to large, industrial demonstration projects for carbon capture. Recovery Act funding for CCPI and ICCS projects was 40% of the *total* amount of funding for all CCS RD&D from FY2008 through FY2012 (**Table 1**). If funding for FutureGen—which is arguably a large CCS demonstration project—were added, then funding for demonstration projects would comprise approximately 58% of the total amount allocated for CCS RD&D over the past five years.

This shift in emphasis to the demonstration phase of carbon capture technology is not surprising, and appears to heed recommendations from many experts who called for large, industrial-scale carbon capture demonstration projects.[22] Primarily, the call for large-scale CCS demonstration projects that capture 1 million metric tons or more of CO_2 per year reflects the need to reduce the additional costs to the power plant or industrial facility associated with capturing the CO_2 before it is emitted to the atmosphere. The capture component of CCS is the costliest component, according to most experts.[23] The higher costs of power plants with CCS, compared to plants without CCS, and the uncertainty in cost estimates results in part from a dearth of information about outstanding technical questions in carbon capture technology at the industrial scale.[24]

In comparative studies of cost estimates for other environmental technologies, such as for power plant scrubbers that remove sulfur and nitrogen compounds from power plant emissions (SO_2 and NOx), some experts note that the farther away a technology is from commercial reality, the more uncertain is its estimated cost. At the beginning of the RD&D process, initial cost estimates could be low, but could typically increase through the demonstration phase before decreasing after successful deployment and commercialization. **Figure 1** shows a cost estimate curve of this type.

---

[21] DOE 2010 *CCS Roadmap*, p. 12.

[22] See, for example, the presentations given by Edward Rubin of Carnegie Mellon University, Howard Herzog of the Massachusetts Institute of Technology, and Jeff Phillips of the Electric Power Research Institute, at the CRS seminar *Capturing Carbon for Climate Control What's in the Toolbox and What's Missing*, November 18, 2009. (Presentations available from Peter Folger at 7-1517.) Rubin stated that at least 10 full-scale demonstration projects would be needed to establish the reliability and true cost of CCS in power plant applications. Herzog also called for at least 10 demonstration plants worldwide that capture and sequester a million metric tons of CO_2 per year. In his presentation, Phillips stated that large-scale demonstrations are critical to building confidence among power plant owners.

[23] For example, an MIT report estimated that the costs of capture could be 80% or more of the total CCS costs. John Deutsch et al., *The Future of Coal*, Massachusetts Institute of Technology, An Interdisciplinary MIT Study, 2007, Executive Summary, p. xi.

[24] *The Future of Coal*, p. 97.

Table 1. DOE Carbon Capture and Storage Research, Development, and Demonstration Program Areas

(funding in $ thousands, FY2008-FY2013)

Program	FY2008	FY2009	Recovery Act	FY2010	Restructured Program after FY2010[a]	FY2011	FY2012 (enacted)	Totals (FY2008-FY2012)	FY2013 (request)
FutureGen	72,262	0	1,000,000	0	FutureGen 2.0	0	0	**1,072,262**	0
Clean Coal Power Initiative (CCPI)	67,444	288,174	800,000	0	CCS Demonstrations	0	0	**1,155,618**	0
Industrial Carbon Capture and Storage Projects			1,520,000	0		0	0	**1,520,000**	0
Site Characterization, Training, Program Direction			80,000	0		0	0	**80,000**	0
Innovations for Existing Plants (IEP)	35,083	48,600	—	50,630	Carbon Capture Research	58,703	68,898	**261,914**	60,438
Advanced Integrated Gasification Combined Cycle (IGCC)	52,029	63,409	—	61,341	Advanced Energy Systems (IGCC)	78,338	54,942	**310,059**	42,604
Advanced Turbines (Hydrogen Turbines)	23,125	27,216	—	31,158	Advanced Energy Systems (Hydrogen Turbines)	30,106	15,000	**126,605**	12,589
Carbon Sequestration (Greenhouse Gas Control)	105,985	132,192	—	136,313	Carbon Storage Research	111,195	105,684	**591,369**	85,751

Carbon Capture and Sequestration: Research, Development, and Demonstration at DOE

Program	FY2008	FY2009	Recovery Act	FY2010	Restructured Program after FY2010[a]	FY2011	FY2012 (enacted)	Totals (FY2008-FY2012)	FY2013 (request)
Carbon Sequestration (Focus Area for CCS Research)	9,635	13,608	—	13,631	**Carbon Storage (Focus Area for CCS Research)**	9,717	9,726	**56,317**	9,726
Fuels (Hydrogen from Coal/Coal to Liquids)	24,088	24,300	—	24,341	**Advanced Energy Systems (Hydrogen from Coal/Coal to Liquids)**	11,661	5,000	**89,390**	0
Solid State Energy Conversion Fuel Cells	53,956	56,376	—	48,683	**Advanced Energy Systems (Fuel Cells)**	48,522	25,000	**232,537**	0
Advanced Research	36,264	27,389	—	27,388	**Cross Cutting Research**	41,446	49,134	**181,621**	29,750
					NETL Coal Research and Development	0	35,011	**35,011**	35,011
Totals	**479,871**	**681,264**	**3,400,000**	**393,485**		**389,688**	**368,395**	**5,712,703**	**275,869**

Source: U.S. Department of Energy, FY2013 Congressional Budget Request, volume 3, Fossil Energy Research and Development, http://www.cfo.doe.gov/budget/13budget/Content/Volume3.pdf; U.S. Department of Energy, Carbon Sequestration, Recovery Act, http://www.fe.doe.gov/recovery/index.html.

Notes: Advanced Energy Systems excludes funding for Hydrogen from Coal, Coal and Coal-Biomass to Liquids, and So id Oxide Fuel Cells programs.

a. In FY2010, post-combustion carbon capture research was included in the Carbon Sequestration (Greenhouse Gas Control) line item, to reflect the transition to a new budget structure proposed for FY2012. This table attempts to show the broad program areas for CCS RD&D before and after the DOE changed the budget structure after FY2010.

Figure 1. Typical Trend in Cost Estimates for a New Technology As It Develops from a Research Concept to Commercial Maturity

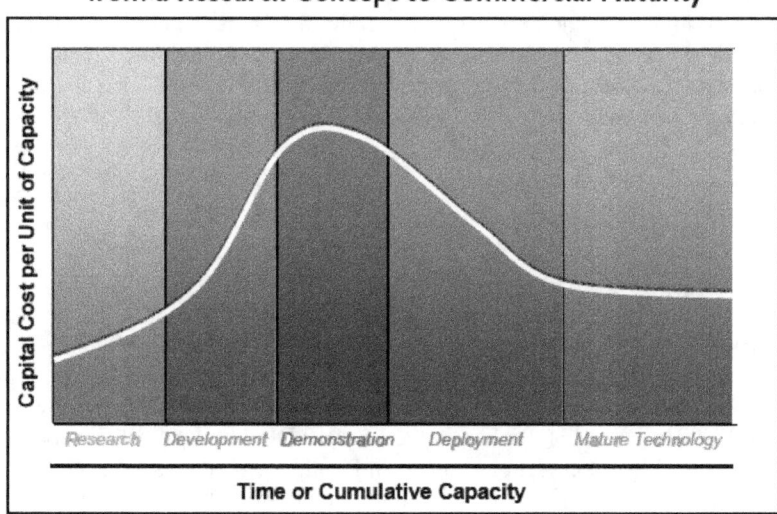

Source: Adapted from S. Dalton, "CO_2 Capture at Coal Fired Power Plants—Status and Outlook," 9th International Conference on Greenhouse Gas Control Technologies, Washington, DC, November, 16-20, 2008.

Deploying commercial-scale CCS demonstration projects—an emphasis within the DOE CCS RD&D program—would therefore provide cost estimates closer to operational conditions rather than laboratory- or pilot-plant-scale projects. In the case of SO_2 and NOx scrubbers, efforts typically took two decades or more to bring new concepts (such as combined SO_2 and NOx capture systems) to the commercial stage. As **Figure 1** indicates, costs for new technologies tend to fall over time with successful deployment and commercialization. It would be reasonable to expect a similar trend for CO_2 capture costs if the technologies become widely deployed.[25]

Recovery Act Funding for CCS Projects: A Lynchpin for Success?

The bulk of Recovery Act funds for CCS ($3.32 billion, or 98%) was directed to three programs: Clean Coal Power Initiative; Industrial Carbon Capture and Storage Projects, and FutureGen (**Table 1**). Under the 2010 *CCS Roadmap*, and with the large infusion of funding from the Recovery Act, DOE's goal is to develop the technologies to allow for commercial-scale demonstration in both new and retrofitted power plants and industrial facilities by 2020. The DOE 2011 *Strategic Plan* sets a more specific target: bring at least five commercial-scale CCS demonstration projects online by 2016.[26]

---

[25] For a fuller discussion of the relationship between costs of developing technologies analogous to CCS, such as SO_2 and NOx scrubbers, see CRS Report R41325, *Carbon Capture A Technology Assessment*, by Peter Folger.

[26] U.S. Department of Energy, *Strategic Plan*, May 2011, p. 18, http://energy.gov/sites/prod/files/2011_DOE_Strategic_Plan_.pdf.

It could be argued that in its allocation of Recovery Act funding, DOE was heeding the recommendations of experts (see footnote 22) who identified commercial-scale demonstration projects as the most important component, the lynchpin, for future development and deployment of CCS in the United States. It could also be argued that much of the future success of CCS is riding on these three programs. Accordingly, the following section provides a snapshot of the CCPI, ICCS, and FutureGen programs, and a brief discussion of some of their accomplishments and challenges.

Clean Coal Power Initiative

The CCPI was an ongoing program prior to the $800 million funding increase from the Recovery Act (see **Table 1**). Recovery Act funding now is being used to expand activities in CCPI Round 3 beyond developing technologies to reduce sulfur, nitrogen, and mercury pollutants from power plants.[27] After enactment of the Recovery Act, DOE did not request additional funding for CCPI under its Fossil Energy program in the annual appropriations process (**Table 1** shows zeroes in the columns for FY2010-FY2013). Rather, in the FY2010 DOE budget justification, DOE stated that funding for the CCPI demonstration projects in Round 3 would be supported through the Recovery Act, and as a result "DOE will make dramatic progress in demonstrating CCS at commercial scale using these funds without the need for additional resources for demonstration in 2010."[28]

According to the 2010 DOE *CCS Roadmap*, Recovery Act funds are being used for CCPI demonstration projects to "allow researchers broader CCS commercial-scale experience by expanding the range of technologies, applications, fuels, and geologic formations that are being tested."[29] DOE selected six projects under CCPI Round 3 through two separate solicitations.[30] The total DOE share of funding would have been $1.54 billion for the six projects in five states: Texas, California, North Dakota, West Virginia, and Alabama (**Table 2**). However, the projects in Alabama, North Dakota, and West Virginia withdrew from the program, and currently the DOE share for the remaining three projects is $881 million (of a total of over $6 billion for total expected costs). With the withdrawal of three CCPI Round 3 projects, DOE's share of the total program costs shrank from nearly 20% to approximately 13%.

---

[27] DOE had solicited and awarded funding for CCPI projects in two previous rounds of funding: CCPI Round 1 and Round 2. The Recovery Act funds were to be allocated CCPI Round 3, focusing on projects that utilize CCS technology and/or the beneficial reuse of CO_2. For more details, see http://www.fossil.energy.gov/programs/powersystems/cleancoal/.

[28] U.S. Department of Energy, *Detailed Budget Justifications FY2010*, volume 7, Fossil Energy Research and Development, p. 35, http://www.cfo.doe.gov/budget/10budget/Content/Volumes/Volume7.pdf.

[29] DOE 2010 *CCS Roadmap*, p. 15.

[30] The first solicitation closing date was January 20, 2009; the second solicitation closing date was August 24, 2009. Thus the first set of project proposals were submitted prior to enactment of the Recovery Act. See http://www.fossil.energy.gov/programs/powersystems/cleancoal/.

Table 2. DOE CCPI Round 3 Projects

CCPI Round 3 Project	Location	DOE Share of Funding ($ millions)	Total Project Cost ($ millions)	Percent DOE Share	Metric Tons of CO$_2$ Captured Annually (millions)	Project Status
Texas Clean Energy Project	Penwell, TX	450	1,727	26%	2.7	Active
Hydrogen Energy California Project	Kern County, CA	408	4,008	10%	1.8 or 2.5	Active
NRG Energy Project	Thompsons, TX	167	334	50%	0.4	Active
AEP Mountaineer Project	New Haven, WV	334	668	50%	1.5	Withdrawn
Southern Company Project	Mobile, AL	295	665	44%	1	Withdrawn
Basin Electric Power Project	Beulah, ND	100	387	26%	0.9	Withdrawn
Total		**1,541**	**7,789**	**19.8%**	**8.3**	
Total, Active Projects[a]		**812**	**6,069**	**13.4%**	**4.9**	

Source: DOE Fossil Energy Tech ine; Environment News Service (March 12, 2010), http://www.ens-newswire.com/ens/mar2010/2010-03-12-093.html; NETL CCPI website, http://www.netl.doe.gov/technologies/coalpower/cctc/ccpi/index.html.

Notes: DOE funding for the NRG Energy Project was initially announced as up to $154 mil ion (see March 9, 2009, DOE Tech ine, http://www.fossil.energy.gov/news/techlines/2010/10005-NRG_Energy_Selected_to_Receive_DOE.html). A May 2010 DOE fact sheet indicates that funding for NRG is $167 million (http://www.netl.doe.gov/pub ications/factsheets/project/FE0003311.pdf).

a.   Total include amounts that were reallocated from withdrawn projects to active projects.

Reasons for Withdrawal from the CCPI Program

Southern Company—Plant Barry 160 MW Project

Southern Company withdrew its Alabama Plant Barry project from the CCPI program on February 22, 2010, slightly more than two months after DOE Secretary Chu announced $295 million in DOE funding for the 11-year, $665 million project that would have captured up to 1 million tons of CO$_2$ per year from a 160 megawatt coal-fired generation unit.[31] According to some sources, Southern Company's decision was based on concern about the size of the company's needed commitment (approximately $350 million) to the project, and its need for more time to perform due diligence on its financial commitment, among other reasons.[32] Southern Company continues work on a much smaller CCS project that would capture CO$_2$ from a 25 MW unit at Plant Barry.

---

[31] MIT Carbon Capture & Sequestration Technologies, *Plant Barry Fact Sheet Carbon Dioxide Capture and Storage Project*, http://sequestration.mit.edu/tools/projects/plant_barry.html.

[32] Ibid.

Basin Electric Power—Antelope Valley 120 MW Project

On July 1, 2009, Secretary Chu announced $100 million in DOE funding for a project that would capture approximately 1 million tons of CO_2 per year from a 120 MW electric-equivalent gas stream from the Antelope Valley power station near Beulah, ND.[33] In December 2010, the Basin Electric Power Cooperative withdrew its project from the CCPI program, citing both regulatory uncertainty with regard to capturing CO_2 and uncertainty about the project's cost (one source indicates that the company estimated $500 million total cost; DOE estimated $387 million—see **Table 2**).[34] The project would have supplied the captured CO_2 to an existing pipeline that transports CO_2 from the Great Plains Synfuels Plant near Beulah for enhanced oil recovery in Canada's Weyburn field approximately 200 miles north in Saskatchewan.

American Electric Power—Mountaineer 235 MW Project

The most recent cancellation was announced in July 2011, when American Electric Power decided to halt its plans to build a carbon capture plant for a 235 MW generation unit at its 1.3 gigawatt Mountaineer power plant in New Haven, WV. The project represented Phase 2 of an ongoing CCPI project. Secretary Chu had earlier announced a $334 million award for the project on December 4, 2009.[35] According to some sources, AEP dropped the project because the company was not certain that state regulators would allow it to recover the additional costs for the CCS project through rate increases charged to its customers.[36] In addition, company officials cited broader economic and policy conditions as reasons for cancelling the project.[37] Some commentators suggested that congressional inaction on setting limits on greenhouse gas emissions, as well as the weak economy, may have diminished the incentives for a company like AEP to invest in CCS.[38] One source concluded that "Phase 2 has been cancelled due to unknown climate policy."[39]

Reshuffling of Funding for CCPI

According to DOE, $140 million of the $295 million previously allotted to the Southern Company Plant Barry project was divided between the Texas Clean Energy project and the Hydrogen Energy California project, together with additional DOE funding, so that each project received an additional $100 million total above its initial awards.[40] The remaining funding from

---

[33] U.S. DOE, Fossil Energy Techline, *Secretary Chu Announces Two New Projects to Reduce Emissions from Coal Plants*, July 1, 2009, http://www.fossil.energy.gov/news/techlines/2009/09043-DOE_Announces_CCPI_Projects.html.

[34] Lauren Donovan, "Basin Shelves Lignite's First Carbon Capture Project," *Bismarck Tribune*, December 17, 2010, http://bismarcktribune.com/news/local/a5fb7ed8-0a1b-11e0-b0ea-001cc4c03286.html.

[35] U.S. DOE, Fossil Energy Techline, *Secretary Chu Announces $3 Billion Investment for Carbon Capture and Sequestration*, December 4, 2009, http://www.fossil.energy.gov/news/techlines/2009/09081-Secretary_Chu_Announces_CCS_Invest.html.

[36] Matthew L. Wald and John M. Broder, "Utility Shelves Ambitious Plan to Limit Carbon," *New York Times*, July 13, 2011, http://www.nytimes.com/2011/07/14/business/energy-environment/utility-shelves-plan-to-capture-carbon-dioxide.html?_r=1.

[37] Michael G. Morris, chairman of AEP, quoted in *New York Times* article by Wald and Broder, July 13, 2011.

[38] Wald and Broder, *New York Times*, July 13, 2011.

[39] MIT Carbon Capture & Sequestration Technologies, *AEP Mountaineer Fact Sheet Carbon Dioxide Capture and Storage Project*, http://sequestration.mit.edu/tools/projects/aep_alstom_mountaineer.html.

[40] Telephone conversation with Joseph Giove, DOE Office of Fossil Energy, March 19, 2012.

---

the canceled Plant Barry project (up to $154 million) was allotted to the NRG Energy project in Texas (see **Table 2**).[41]

According to a DOE source, selection of the Basin Electric Power project was announced but a cooperative agreement was never awarded by DOE.[42] Funds that were to be obligated for the Basin project could therefore have been reallocated within the department, but were rescinded by Congress in FY2011 appropriations.

Some of the funding for the AEP Mountaineer project was rescinded by Congress in FY2012 appropriations legislation (P.L. 112-74). In the report accompanying P.L. 112-74, Congress rescinded a total of $187 million of prior-year balances from the Fossil Energy Research and Development account.[43] The rescission did not apply to amounts previously appropriated under P.L. 111-5; however, funding for the AEP Mountaineer project that was provided by the Recovery Act and not spent was returned to the Treasury and not made available to the CCPI program.[44]

Industrial Carbon Capture and Storage Projects

The original DOE ICCS program was divided into two main areas: Area 1, consisting of large industrial demonstration projects; and Area 2, consisting of projects to test innovative concepts for the beneficial reuse of CO_2.[45] Under Area 1, the first phase of the program consisted of 12 projects cost-shared with private industry, intended to increase investment in clean industrial technologies and sequestration projects. Phase I projects averaged approximately seven months in duration. Following Phase I, DOE selected three projects for Phase 2 for design, construction, and operation.[46] The three Phase 2 projects are listed as large-scale demonstration projects in **Table 3**. The total share of DOE funding for the three projects, provided by the Recovery Act, is $686 million, or approximately 64% of the sum total Area 1 program cost of $1.075 billion.

Under Area 2, the initial phase consisted of $17.4 million in Recovery Act funding and $7.7 million in private-sector funding for 12 projects to engage in feasibility studies to examine the beneficial reuse of CO_2.[47] In July 2010, DOE selected 6 projects from the original 12 projects for a second phase of funding to find ways of converting captured CO_2 into useful products such as fuel, plastics, cement, and fertilizer. The 6 projects are listed under "Innovative Concepts/Beneficial Use" in **Table 3**. The total share of DOE funding for the 6 projects, provided by the Recovery Act, is $141.5 million, or approximately 71% of the sum total cost of $198.2 million.

---

[41] U.S. DOE Fossil Energy Techline, "Secretary Chu Announces Up To $154 Million for NRG Energy's Carbon Capture and Storage Project in Texas," March 9, 2010, http://www.fossil.energy.gov/news/techlines/2010/10005-NRG_Energy_Selected_to_Receive_DOE.html.

[42] Telephone conversation with Joseph Giove, DOE Office of Fossil Energy, April 11, 2011.

[43] U.S. Congress, House Committee on Appropriations, Subcommittee on Military Construction, Veterans Affairs, and Related Agencies, *Military Construction and Veterans Affairs and Related Agencies Appropriations Act, 2012*, conference report to accompany H.R. 2055, 112th Cong., 1st sess., December 15, 2011, H.Rept. 112-331 (Washington: GPO, 2011), p. 851.

[44] Telephone conversation with Joseph Giove, DOE Office of Fossil Energy, March 19, 2012.

[45] Email from Regis K. Conrad, Director, Division of Cross-Cutting Research, DOE, March 20, 2012.

[46] U.S. DOE, National Energy Technology Laboratory, *Major Demonstrations, Industrial Capture and Storage (ICCS) Area 1*, http://www.netl.doe.gov/technologies/coalpower/cctc/iccs1/index.html#.

[47] U.S. DOE, *Recovery Act, Innovative Concepts for Beneficial Reuse of Carbon Dioxide*, http://fossil.energy.gov/recovery/projects/beneficial_reuse.html.

Table 3. DOE Industrial Carbon Capture and Storage (ICCS) Projects

(showing DOE share of funding and total project cost)

ICCS Project Name	Location	Type of Project	DOE Share of Funding ($ millions)	Total Project Cost ($ millions)	Percent DOE Share
Air Products & Chemicals, Inc.	Port Arthur, TX	Large-Scale Demonstration	284	431	66%
Archer Daniels Midland Co.	Decatur, IL	Large-Scale Demonstration	141	208	68%
Leucadia Energy, LLC	Lake Charles, LA	Large-Scale Demonstration	261	436	60%
Alcoa, Inc.	Alcoa Center, PA	Innovative Concepts/Beneficial Use	13.5	16.9	80%
Novomer, Inc.	Ithaca, NY	Innovative Concepts/Beneficial Use	20.5	25.6	80%
Touchstone Research Lab, Ltd.	Triadelphia, PA	Innovative Concepts/Beneficial Use	6.7	8.4	80%
Phycal, LLC	Highland Heights, OH	Innovative Concepts/Beneficial Use	51.4	65	80%
Skyonic Corp.	Austin, TX	Innovative Concepts/Beneficial Use	28	39.6	70%
Calera Corp.	Los Gatos, CA	Innovative Concepts/Beneficial Use	21.4	42.7	50%
Air Products & Chemicals, Inc.	Allentown, PA	Advanced Gasification Technologies	71.7	75	96%
Eltron Research & Development, Inc.	Boulder, CO	Advanced Gasification Technologies	71.4	73.7	97%
Research Triangle Institute	Research Triangle Park, NC	Advanced Gasification Technologies	168.8	174	97%
GE Energy	Schenectady, NY	Advanced Turbo-Machinery	31.3	62.6	50%
Siemens Energy	Orlando, FL	Advanced Turbo-Machinery	32.3	64.7	50%
Clean Energy Systems, Inc.	Rancho Cordova, CA	Advanced Turbo-Machinery	30	42.9	70%
Ramgen Power Systems	Bellevue, WA	Advanced Turbo-Machinery	50	79.7	63%
ADA-ES, Inc.	Littleton, CO	Post-Combustion Capture	15	18.8	80%
Alstom Power	Windsor, CT	Post-Combustion Capture	10	12.5	80%
Membrane Technology & Research, Inc.	Menlo Park, CA	Post-Combustion Capture	15	18.8	80%

ICCS Project Name	Location	Type of Project	DOE Share of Funding ($ millions)	Total Project Cost ($ millions)	Percent DOE Share
Praxair	Tonawanda, NY	Post-Combustion Capture	35	55.6	63%
Siemens Energy, Inc.	Pittsburgh, PA	Post-Combustion Capture	15	18.8	80%
Board of Trustees U. of IL	Champaign, IL	Geologic Site Characterization	5	6.5	77%
N. American Power Group, Ltd.	Greenwood Village, CO	Geologic Site Characterization	5	7.85	64%
Sandia Technologies, LLC	Houston, TX	Geologic Site Characterization	4.38	5.63	78%
S. Carolina Research Foundation	Columbia, SC	Geologic Site Characterization	5	6.25	80%
Terralog Technologies USA, Inc.	Arcadia, CA	Geologic Site Characterization	5	6.25	80%
U. of Alabama	Tuscaloosa, AL	Geologic Site Characterization	5	10.8	46%
U. of Kansas Center for Research, Inc.	Lawrence, KS	Geologic Site Characterization	5	6.29	80%
U. of Texas at Austin	Austin, TX	Geologic Site Characterization	5	6.25	80%
U. of Utah	Salt Lake City, UT	Geologic Site Characterization	5	7.23	69%
U. of Wyoming	Laramie, WY	Geologic Site Characterization	5	5	100%
		Totals	**1,422.4**	**2,038.4**	**70%**

Source: Emails from Regis K. Conrad, Director, Division of Cross-Cutting Research, DOE, March 20 and March 27, 2012; U.S. DOE, National Energy Technology Laboratory, *Major Demonstrations, Industrial Capture and Storage (ICCS): Area 1*, http://www.netl.doe.gov/technologies/coalpower/cctc/iccs1/index.html#; U.S. DOE, *Carbon Capture and Storage from Industrial Sources, Industrial Carbon Capture Project Selections*, http://fossil.energy.gov/recovery/projects/iccs_projects_0907101.pdf.

Notes: Table is ordered from top to bottom by type of project: Large-Scale Demonstration; Innovative Concepts/Beneficial Use; Advanced Gasification Technologies; Advanced Turbo-Machinery; Post-Combustion Capture; and Geologic Site Characterization. Totals may not add due to rounding.

Since its original conception, the DOE ICCS program has expanded with an additional 22 projects, funded under the Recovery Act, to accelerate promising technologies for CCS.[48] In its listing of the 22 projects, DOE groups them into four general categories: (1) Large-Scale Testing of Advanced Gasification Technologies; (2) Advanced Turbo-Machinery to Lower Emissions

---

[48] Email from Regis K. Conrad, Director, Division of Cross-Cutting Research, DOE, March 20, 2012.

from Industrial Sources; (3) Post-Combustion CO_2 Capture with Increased Efficiencies and Decreased Costs; and (4) Geologic Storage Site Characterization.[49] The total share of DOE funding for the 22 projects, provided by Recovery Act, is $594.9 million, or approximately 78% of the sum total cost of $765.2 million.

Overall, the total share of federal funding for all the ICCS projects combined is $1.422 billion, or approximately 70% of the sum total cost of $2.038 billion.

FutureGen—A Special Case?

Brief History Since 2003

On February 27, 2003, President Bush proposed a 10-year, $1 billion project to build a coal-fired power plant that would integrate carbon sequestration and hydrogen production while producing 275 megawatts of electricity, enough to power about 150,000 average U.S. homes. As originally conceived, the plant would have been a coal-gasification facility and would have produced and sequestered between 1 million and 2 million tons of CO_2 annually. On January 30, 2008, DOE announced that it was "restructuring" the FutureGen program away from a single, state-of-the-art "living laboratory" of integrated R&D technologies—a single plant—to instead pursue a new strategy of multiple commercial demonstration projects.[50] In the restructured program, DOE would support up to two or three demonstration projects of at least 300 megawatts that would sequester at least 1 million tons of CO_2 per year.

In the Bush Administration's FY2009 budget, DOE requested $156 million for the restructured FutureGen program, and specified that the federal cost-share would only cover the CCS portions of the demonstration projects, not the entire power system. However, after the Recovery Act was enacted on February 17, 2009, Secretary Chu announced an agreement with the FutureGen Alliance—an industry consortium—to advance construction of the FutureGen plant built in Mattoon, IL, the site selected by the FutureGen Alliance in 2007.[51] Further, DOE anticipated that $1 billion of funding from the Recovery Act would be used to support the project.[52]

On August 5, 2010, Secretary Chu announced the $1 billion award, from Recovery Act funds, to the FutureGen Alliance, Ameren Energy Resources, Babcock & Wilcox, and Air Liquide Process & Construction, Inc., to build FutureGen 2.0.[53] FutureGen 2.0 differs from the original concept for the plant, because it would retrofit Ameren's existing power plant in Meridosia, IL, with oxy-combustion technology at a 202 MW, oil-fired unit,[54] rather than build a new state-of-the-art plant

---

[49] U.S. DOE, Carbon Capture and Storage from Industrial Sources, Industrial Carbon Capture Project Selections, http://fossil.energy.gov/recovery/projects/iccs_projects_0907101.pdf.

[50] See http://www.fossil.energy.gov/news/techlines/2008/08003-DOE_Announces_Restructured_FutureG.html.

[51] Prior to when DOE first announced it would restructure the program in 2008, the FutureGen Alliance announced on December 18, 2007, that it had selected Mattoon, IL, as the host site from a set of four finalists. The four were Mattoon, IL; Tuscola, IL; Heart of Brazos (near Jewett, TX); and Odessa, TX.

[52] See DOE announcement on June 12, 2009, http://www.fossil.energy.gov/news/techlines/2009/09037-DOE_Announces_FutureGen_Agreement.html.

[53] See DOE Techline, http://www.netl.doe.gov/publications/press/2010/10033-Secretary_Chu_Announces_FutureGen_.html.

[54] Ameren had planned to replace the oil-fired boiler with a coal-fired boiler using oxy-combustion technology to allow carbon capture. See http://www.futuregenalliance.org/pdf/FutureGen%20FAQ-General%20042711.pdf.

in Mattoon. DOE announced that Mattoon would serve as the storage site for the CO_2 captured in Meridosia, and the two sites would be connected by a CO_2 pipeline to transport the gas.

The choice of Mattoon as the storage site met with opposition from the community in Coles County, IL, which includes the town of Mattoon. A group representing business development in Coles County sent a letter to Senator Dick Durbin (IL) stating that the community did not wish to be part of the new FutureGen 2.0 project with the Mattoon site solely as a storage facility.[55] Subsequently, DOE and the FutureGen Alliance announced details of the process for selecting a new storage site in Illinois that would receive and store the 1 million or more metric tons of CO_2 from the Meridosia plant, and possibly CO_2 from other sources.[56] On February 28, 2011, the FutureGen Alliance announced that it had selected Morgan County, IL, as the location for the storage site.[57] Morgan County is west of Springfield, IL, and north of St. Louis, MO. Meridosia Unit 4, which would be repowered and retrofitted with a coal oxy-combustion carbon capture unit under FutureGen 2.0, is located about 20 miles west of Springfield.[58]

Current Status

The FutureGen 2.0 project has two parts: oxy-combustion carbon capture technology, implemented through a cooperative agreement with Ameren Energy Resources and industrial partners; and a pipeline and regional CO_2 storage reservoir project, implemented through a cooperative agreement with the FutureGen Alliance.[59] In addition to the $1 billion provided under the Recovery Act for the overall FutureGen 2.0 project, $53.6 million of prior appropriations would be provided for the pipeline and regional CO_2 storage portion. For the oxy-combustion carbon capture technology portion, DOE would provide $589.7 million, or 80%, of the $737 million in total costs. For the pipeline and regional CO_2 storage portion, DOE would provide $458.6 million, or 83%, of the $553 million in total costs.[60] The total federal and private-sector costs for FutureGen 2.0 are estimated to be almost $1.3 billion. The federal funding was formally awarded on October 1, 2010, and the award ends on December 31, 2020.

Challenges to FutureGen—A Similar Path for Other Demonstration Projects?

Slightly over a year after Secretary Chu announced the Recovery Act-funded award for FutureGen 2.0, Ameren Energy announced it was closing the Meridosia power plant, citing

---

[55] Environmental News Service, "Future Unclear for FutureGen 2.0 Carbon Capture and Storage Network," August 17, 2010, http://www.ens-newswire.com/ens/aug2010/2010-08-17-093.html. Also, see David Mercer, "Ill. Town Rejects Changes to Federal FutureGen Coal Project, Backs Out After More Than Two Years," *Associated Press*, August 11, 2010, http://www.startribune.com/templates/Print_This_Story?sid=100479394.

[56] DOE Techline, *FutureGen Industrial Alliance Announces Carbon Storage Site Selection Process for FutureGen 2.0*, http://www.fossil.energy.gov/news/techlines/2010/10051-FutureGen_Site_Selection_Process_A.html.

[57] FutureGen Alliance, "FutureGen Alliance Selects Morgan County, Ill. as the Site for the FutureGen 2.0 Carbon Storage Facility," February 28, 2011, http://www.futuregenalliance.org/pdf/pr_02_28_11.pdf. In its announcement, the FutureGen Alliance notes that it selected Christian County and Douglas County as alternative sites in case of concerns over the Morgan County selection.

[58] NETL factsheet, *FutureGen 2.0*, http://www.netl.doe.gov/publications/factsheets/project/FE0001882-FE0005054.pdf.

[59] Ibid.

[60] Ibid.

---

additional costs imposed by the requirement for environmental controls mandated by EPA under the authority of the Clean Air Act.[61] Ameren initially stated that the closure would not affect plans for FutureGen 2.0; however, it later reportedly admitted that it could not participate in the project.[62] The FutureGen Alliance subsequently entered into negotiations seeking to purchase parts of the Meridosia power plant from Ameren, which would likely allow the project to move forward and bring the generating unit retrofitted with oxy-combustion technology into production in 2016.[63]

In addition to the challenges of securing private-sector financing, acquiring the generating unit from Ameren, retrofitting it with oxy-combustion technology to capture 90% of the CO_2 emitted, and building a pipeline to a storage site, the project faces other potential hurdles. The FutureGen Alliance will need to secure approval for a specific storage site in Morgan County, which would also involve acquiring rights from private landowners to store the captured CO_2 in underground pore space, in addition to leasing the surface to build the infrastructure for injecting the CO_2 underground. As those decisions draw closer, past experience suggests that some local opposition to injecting and storing CO_2 indefinitely in the subsurface could emerge, and could derail the project unless a consensus within the local community is achieved.[64]

A question for Congress is whether FutureGen represents a unique case of a first mover in a complex, expensive, and technically challenging endeavor, or whether it represents all large CCS demonstration projects once they move past the planning stage. As discussed above, approximately $3.3 billion of Recovery Act funding is committed to large demonstration projects, including FutureGen. A rationale for committing such a substantial level of funding to demonstration projects was to scale up CCS RD&D more quickly than had been the pace of technology development prior to enactment of the Recovery Act. However, if all the CCS demonstration projects encounter similar changes in scope, design, location, and cost as FutureGen, the chances of meeting goals laid out in the DOE 2010 *Strategic Plan*—namely, to bring at least five commercial-scale CCS demonstration projects online by 2016—may be in jeopardy.

Alternatively, one could argue that FutureGen from its original conception was unique. None of the other large-scale demonstration projects share the same original ambitious vision: to create a new, one-of-a-kind, CCS plant from the ground up. Even though the individual components of FutureGen—as originally conceived—were not themselves new innovations, combining the capture, transportation, and storage components together into a 250-megawatt functioning power plant could be considered unprecedented and therefore most likely to experience delays at each step in development.

---

[61] "Ameren Will Shutter 2 Ill. Plants," *Greenwire*, October 4, 2011, http://www.eenews.net/Greenwire/2011/10/04/archive/12?terms=futuregen.

[62] Matthew Wald, "Coal Project Hits Snag as a Partner Backs Off," *New York Times*, November 10, 2011, http://www.nytimes.com/2011/11/11/business/energy-environment/coal-project-hits-snag-as-a-partner-backs-off.html?_r=1.

[63] Gabriel Nelson, "FutureGen in Talks to Buy Ill. Power Plant for CCS Pilot Project," *Greenwire*, November 28, 2011, http://www.eenews.net/Greenwire/2011/11/28/archive/2?terms=futuregen.

[64] See, for example, the experience in Germany by Swedish power utility Vattenfall, which recently cancelled plans to build a CCS power plant because of local opposition to injecting and storing CO_2 underground. Paul Voosen, "Public Outcry Scuttles German Demonstration Plant," *Greenwire*, December 6, 2011, http://www.eenews.net/Greenwire/2011/12/06/archive/10?terms=futuregen.

Scholars have described the stages of technological change in different schemes, such as

- invention, innovation, adoption, diffusion;[65] or

- technology readiness levels (TRLs) ranging from TRL 1 (basic technology research) to TRL 9 (system test, launch, and operations);[66] or

- conceptual design, laboratory/bench scale, pilot plant scale, full-scale demonstration plant, and commercial process.[67]

FutureGen is difficult to categorize within these schemes, in part because the project spanned a range of technology development levels irrespective of the particular scheme. The original conception of the FutureGen project arguably had aspects of conceptual design through commercial processes—all five components of the scheme listed as the third bullet above—which meant that the project was intended to march through all stages in a linear fashion. As some scholars have noted, however, the stages of technological change are highly interactive, requiring learning by doing and learning by using, once the project progresses past its innovative stage into larger-scale demonstration and deployment.[68] The task of tackling all the stages of technology development in one project—the original FutureGen—might have been too daunting and, in addition to other factors, contributed to the project's erratic progress since 2003. It remains to be seen whether the current large-scale demonstration projects funded by DOE under CCPI Round 3 follow the path of FutureGen or instead achieve their technological development goals on time and within their current budgets.[69]

Geologic Sequestration/Storage: DOE RD&D for the Last Step in CCS

DOE has allocated between $115 million and $150 million per year for its carbon sequestration/ storage activities from FY2008 through FY2012, shown in **Table 1** as "Carbon Sequestration (Greenhouse Gas Control)" and "Carbon Sequestration (Focus Area for CCS Research)" for FY2008 through FY2010; and as "Carbon Storage" after FY2010. The total amount allocated to carbon sequestration/carbon storage activities over that five-year period is slightly less than $650 million. In contrast with the carbon capture technology RD&D, which received nearly all of the $3.4 billion from Recovery Act funding, carbon sequestration/carbon storage activities received

---

[65] E. S. Rubin, "The Government Role in Technology Innovation: Lessons for the Climate Change Policy Agenda," Institute of Transportation Studies, 10th Biennial Conference on Transportation Energy and Environmental Policy, University of California, Davis, CA (August 2005).

[66] National Aeronautics and Space Administration, "Definition of Technology Readiness Levels," at http://esto.nasa.gov/files/TRL_definitions.pdf.

[67] For a more thorough discussion of different schemes describing stages of technology development, see chapter 4 of CRS Report R41325, *Carbon Capture A Technology Assessment*, by Peter Folger.

[68] E. S. Rubin, "The Government Role in Technology Innovation: Lessons for the Climate Change Policy Agenda," Institute of Transportation Studies, 10th Biennial Conference on Transportation Energy and Environmental Policy, University of California, Davis, CA (August 2005).

[69] Another possible source of uncertainty for FutureGen, and other large industrial CCS projects, is cost recovery during the operating phase of the plant after the construction phase and initial capital investments are made. "Learning by doing" should increase operating efficiency, but it is unclear by how much and over what time span. For more discussion on cost trajectories and expected efficiency gains, see CRS Report R41325, *Carbon Capture A Technology Assessment*, by Peter Folger.

---

approximately $50 million in Recovery Act funds, or about 7% of the total funding amount for carbon sequestration since FY2008. Recovery Act funds were awarded for 10 projects to conduct site characterization of promising geologic formations for CO_2 storage.[70]

Brief History of DOE Geological Sequestration/Storage Activities

DOE has devoted the bulk of its funding for geological sequestration/storage activities to RD&D efforts for injecting CO_2 into subsurface geological reservoirs. Injection and storage is the third step in the CCS process following the CO_2 capture step and CO_2 transport step. One part of the RD&D effort is characterizing geologic reservoirs (which received a $50 million boost from Recovery Act funds, as noted above); however, the overall program is much broader than just characterization, and has now reached the beginning of the phase of large-volume CO_2 injection demonstration projects across the country. According to DOE, these large-volume tests are needed to validate long-term storage in a variety of different storage formations of different depositional environments, including deep saline reservoirs, depleted oil and gas reservoirs, low permeability reservoirs, coal seams, shale, and basalt.[71] The large-volume tests can be considered injection experiments conducted at a commercial scale (i.e., approximately 1 million tons of CO_2 injected per year) that should provide crucial information on the suitability of different geologic reservoirs; monitoring, verification, and accounting of injected CO_2; risk assessment protocols for long-term injection and storage; and other critical challenges.

In 2003 DOE created seven regional carbon sequestration partnerships (RCSPs), essentially consortia of public and private sector organizations grouped by geographic region across the United States and parts of Canada.[72] The geographic representation was intended to match regional differences in fossil fuel use and geologic reservoir potential for CO_2 storage.[73] The RCSPs cover 43 states and 4 Canadian provinces and include over 400 organizations, according to the DOE 2010 *Strategic Plan*. **Table 4** shows the seven partnerships, the lead organization for each, and the states and provinces included. Several states belong to more than one RCSP.

The RCSPs have pursued their objectives through three phases beginning in 2003:
(1) Characterization Phase (2003 to 2005), an initial examination of the region's potential for geological sequestration of CO_2; (2) Validation Phase (2005 to 2011), small-scale injection field tests (less than 500,000 tons of CO_2) to develop a better understanding of how different geologic formations would handle large amounts of injected CO_2; and (3) Development Phase (2008 to 2018 and beyond), injection tests of at least 1 million tons of CO_2 to simulate commercial-scale quantities of injected CO_2.[74] The last phase is intended also to collect enough information to help understand the regulatory, economic, liability, ownership, and public outreach requirements for commercial deployment of CCS.

---

[70] The total DOE share for the 10 projects is $46.6 million. See DOE, *Recovery Act*, http://fossil.energy.gov/recovery/projects/site_characterization.html.

[71] DOE 2010 *CCS Roadmap*, p. 55.

[72] Four Canadian provinces are partners with DOE in two of the regional partnerships, and are members with other participating organizations that are contributing funding and other support to the partnerships.

[73] DOE National Energy Technology Laboratory, Carbon Sequestration Regional Carbon Sequestration Partnerships, http://www.netl.doe.gov/technologies/carbon_seq/infrastructure/rcsp.html.

[74] Ibid.

Table 4. Regional Carbon Sequestration Partnerships

Regional Carbon Sequestration Partnership (RCSP)	Lead Organization	States and Provinces in the Partnership
Big Sky Carbon Sequestration Partnership (BSCSP)	Montana State University-Bozeman	MT, WY, ID, SD, eastern WA, eastern OR
Midwest Geological Sequestration Consortium (MGSC)	Illinois State Geological Survey	IL, IN, KY
Midwest Regional Carbon Sequestration Partnership (MRCSP)	Battelle Memorial Institute	IN, KY, MD, MI, NJ, NY, OH, PA, WV,
Plains CO$_2$ Reduction Partnership (PCOR)	University of North Dakota Energy and Environmental Research Center	MT, northeast WY, ND, SD, NE, MN, IA, MO, WI, Manitoba, A berta, Saskatchewan, British Columbia (Canada)
Southeast Regional Carbon Sequestration Partnership (SECARB)	Southern States Energy Board	AL, AS, FL, GA, LA, MS, NC, SC, TN, TX, VA, portions of KY and WV
Southwest Regional Partnership on Carbon Sequestration (SWP)	New Mexico Institute of Mining and Technology	AZ, CO, OK, NM, UT, KS, NV, TX, WY
West Coast Regional Carbon Sequestration Partnership (WESTCARB)	California Energy Commission	AK, AZ, CA, HI, OR, NV, WA, British Columbia (Canada)

Source: DOE National Energy Technology Laboratory, *Carbon Sequestration Regional Carbon Sequestration Partnerships*, http://www.netl.doe.gov/technologies/carbon_seq/infrastructure/rcsp.html.

There are RD&D activities funded by DOE under its carbon sequestration/carbon storage program activities other than the RCSPs, such as geological storage technologies; monitoring, verification, and assessment; carbon use and reuse; and others. However, the RCSPs have averaged 50% or more of annual spending on carbon sequestration/carbon storage over the past three years. In the Administration's FY2013 budget request, funding for RCSPs would comprise 70% of the carbon storage research account. The RCSPs provide the framework and infrastructure for a wide variety of DOE geologic sequestration/storage activities.

Current Status and Challenges to Carbon Sequestration/Storage

The third phase—Development—is currently underway for all the RCSPs, and large-scale CO$_2$ injection has begun for the SECARB and MGSC projects.[75] The Development Phase large-scale injection projects are arguably akin to the large-scale carbon capture demonstration projects discussed above. They are needed to understand what actually happens to CO$_2$ underground when commercial-scale volumes are injected in the same or similar geologic reservoirs as would be used if CCS were deployed nationally.

---

[75] For details on the two large-scale injection experiments by SECARB, see http://www.secarbon.org/; for details on the large-scale injection experiment by MGSC, see http://sequestration.org/.

In addition to understanding the technical challenges to storing CO_2 underground without leakage over hundreds of years, DOE also expects that the Development Phase projects will provide a better understanding of regulatory, liability, and ownership issues associated with commercial-scale CCS.[76] These nontechnical issues are not trivial, and could pose serious challenges to widespread deployment of CCS even if the technical challenges of injecting CO_2 safely and in perpetuity are resolved. For example, a complete regulatory framework for managing the underground injection of CO_2 has not been developed in the United States. However, EPA promulgated a rule under the authority of the Safe Drinking Water Act (SDWA) that creates a new class of injection wells under the existing Underground Injection Control Program. The new class of wells (Class VI) establishes national requirements specifically for injecting CO_2 and protecting underground sources of drinking water. EPA's stated purpose in proposing the rule was to ensure that CCS can occur in a safe and effective manner in order to enable commercial-scale CCS to move forward.[77]

The development of the regulation for Class VI wells highlighted that EPA's authority under the SDWA is limited to protecting underground sources of drinking water but does not address other major issues. Some of these include the long-term liability for injected CO_2, regulation of potential emissions to the atmosphere, legal issues if the CO_2 plume migrates underground across state boundaries, private property rights of owners of the surface lands above the injected CO_2 plume, and ownership of the subsurface reservoirs (also referred to as pore space).[78] Because of these issues and others, there are some indications that broad community acceptance of CCS may be a challenge. The large-scale injection tests may help identify the key factors that lead to community concerns over CCS, and help guide DOE, EPA, other agencies, and the private sector towards strategies leading to the widespread deployment of CCS. Currently, however, the general public is largely unfamiliar with the details of CCS and these challenges have yet to be resolved.[79]

Future Outlook

The success of the Clean Coal Program will ultimately be judged by the extent to which emerging technologies get deployed in domestic and international marketplaces. Both technical and financial challenges associated with the deployment of new "high risk" coal technologies must be overcome in order to be capable of achieving success in the marketplace. Commercial scale demonstrations help the industry understand and overcome startup issues, address component integration issues, and gain the early learning commercial experience necessary to reduce risk and secure private financing and investment for future plants.[80]

---

[76] DOE National Energy Technology Laboratory, *Carbon Sequestration Regional Partnership Development Phase (Phase III) Projects*, http://www.netl.doe.gov/technologies/carbon_seq/infrastructure/rcspiii.html.

[77] For more information on the EPA Class VI wells in particular, and the Safe Drinking Water Act generally, see CRS Report RL34201, *Safe Drinking Water Act (SDWA) Selected Regulatory and Legislative Issues*, by Mary Tiemann.

[78] For a discussion of several of these legal issues, see CRS Report RL34307, *Legal Issues Associated with the Development of Carbon Dioxide Sequestration Technology*, by Adam Vann and Paul W. Parfomak.

[79] For more information on the different issues regarding community acceptance of CCS, see CRS Report RL34601, *Community Acceptance of Carbon Capture and Sequestration Infrastructure Siting Challenges*, by Paul W. Parfomak.

[80] Testimony of Scott Klara, Deputy Laboratory Director, National Energy Technology Laboratory, U.S. Department of Energy, in U.S. Congress, Senate Energy and Natural Resources Committee, *Carbon Capture and Sequestration Legislation*, hearing to receive testimony on carbon capture and sequestration legislation, including S. 699 and S. 757, 112th Cong., 1st sess., May 12, 2011, S.Hrg. 112-22.

The testimony quoted above from Scott Klara of the National Energy Technology Laboratory sums up a crucial metric to the success of the federal CCS RD&D program, namely, whether CCS technologies are deployed in the commercial marketplace. To date, there are no commercial ventures in the United States that capture, transport, and inject large quantities of CO_2 (e.g., 1 million tons per year or more) solely for the purposes of carbon sequestration.

However, the CCS RD&D program in 2012 is just now embarking on commercial-scale demonstration projects for CO_2 capture, injection, and storage. The success of these demonstration projects will likely bear heavily on the future outlook for widespread deployment of CCS technologies as a strategy for preventing large quantities of CO_2 from reaching the atmosphere while plants continue to burn fossil fuels, mainly coal. Congress may wish to carefully review the results from these demonstration projects as they progress in order to gauge whether DOE is on track to meet its goal of allowing for an advanced CCS technology portfolio to be ready by 2020 for large-scale demonstration and deployment in the United States.

In addition to the issues and programs discussed above, other factors might affect the demonstration and deployment of CCS in the United States. The use of hydraulic fracturing techniques to extract unconventional natural gas deposits recently has drawn national attention to the possible negative consequences of deep well injection of large volumes of fluids. Hydraulic fracturing involves the high-pressure injection of fluids into the target formation to fracture the rock and release natural gas or oil. The injected fluids, together with naturally occurring fluids in the shale, are referred to as produced water. Produced waters are pumped out of the well and disposed of. Often the produced waters are disposed of by re-injecting them at a different site in a different well. These practices have raised concerns about possible leakage as fluids are pumped into and out of the ground, and about deep well injection causing earthquakes. Public concerns over hydraulic fracturing and deep-well injection of produced waters may spill over into concerns about deep-well injection of CO_2. How successfully DOE is able to address these types of concerns as the large-scale demonstration projects move forward into their injection phases could affect the future of CCS deployment.

Author Contact Information

Peter Folger
Specialist in Energy and Natural Resources Policy
pfolger@crs.loc.gov, 7-1517